# DIMETRODON

For a free color catalog describing Gareth Stevens Publishing's list of high-quality
books and multimedia programs, call 1-800-542-2595 (USA) or 1-800-461-9120 (Canada).
Gareth Stevens Publishing's Fax: (414) 225-0377.
See our catalog, too, on the World Wide Web: http://gsinc.com

**Library of Congress Cataloging-in-Publication Data**

Green, Tamara, 1945-
    Dimetrodon / by Tamara Green ; illustrated by Tony Gibbons.
      p. cm. — (The extinct species collection)
    Includes index.
    Summary: Describes the physical characteristics and habits of
this prehistoric sail-backed reptile.
    ISBN 0-8368-1589-0 (lib. bdg.)
    1. Dimetrodon—Juvenile literature.  [1. Dimetrodon.
2. Dinosaurs.]  I. Gibbons, Tony, ill.  II. Title.  III. Series.
QE862.P3G74   1996
567.9'3—dc20                        96-5003

First published in North America in 1996 by
**Gareth Stevens Publishing**
1555 North RiverCenter Drive, Suite 201
Milwaukee, Wisconsin 53212 USA

This U.S. edition © 1996 by Gareth Stevens, Inc.  Created with original © 1995 by
Quartz Editorial Services, 112 Station Road, Edgware HA8 7AQ U.K.

Additional artwork by Clare Heronneau

U.S. Editors: Barbara J. Behm, Mary Dykstra

Printed in Mexico

1 2 3 4 5 6 7 8 9 99 98 97 96

the

# EXTINCT SPECIES

collection

# DIMETRODON

## by Tamara Green
### Illustrated by Tony Gibbons

Gareth Stevens Publishing
**MILWAUKEE**

# Contents

# Meet
# Dimetrodon

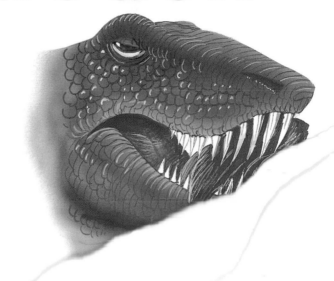

Although it resembled a dinosaur, **Dimetrodon** (DIE-<u>MET</u>-ROE-DON) lived long before the dinosaurs.

What sort of creature, then, was this prehistoric beast? Where did it live, and what did it eat? And, most of all, why did it have that large sail-like structure sticking up from its back?

...at follow, you will ...scinating facts about ...odon as you come face-to-... with this carnivore and other ...rehistoric life forms.

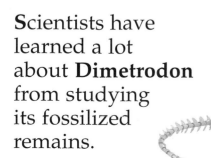

Scientists have learned a lot about **Dimetrodon** from studying its fossilized remains.

# Sail-backed

**Dimetrodon** was a most peculiar reptile! It resembled a huge lizard – topped with that strange, upright structure that grew on its back.

**Dimetrodon** lived in an area that is now the state of Texas. Scientists have found its bones in that region. The animal was about 11 feet (3.3 meters) long when fully grown. That's longer than an average car.

**Dimetrodon**'s "sail" was made of a series of long spines covered with skin. The spines increased in length toward the center of the structure and stood up from the backbone. This structure probably looked much like a ship's sail. Scientists once thought the sail may even have been used to help the reptile cross water. But, as you will find out later in this book, it had an entirely different purpose.

# reptile

After studying the animal's fossilized teeth, experts have also concluded that **Dimetrodon** must have been a carnivore. For food, it probably hunted other reptiles and amphibians (creatures that live on land but breed in water).

Its teeth were long and sharp, particularly those in the front. These teeth would have been ideal for stabbing prey and slicing flesh. The word *Dimetrodon* actually means "two-sized teeth." The animal was given this name because some of its teeth were longer than others.

**Dimetrodon**, as you can see in the illustration, had a long tail and four short, sturdy legs that ended in chunky, five-toed feet.

**Dimetrodon** probably lived on Earth about 100 million years before dinosaurs did.

# Greedy

A terrified shriek pierced the dawn. A hungry **Dimetrodon** had stalked and caught its prey. Early in the day, it had used the sail on its back to warm up. It was well prepared to sneak up on the sluggish, smaller animal. **Dimetrodon** grabbed the **Varanosaurus** (VAH-RAN-OH-SAW-RUS) in its jaws and shook it viciously until, at last, it stopped struggling.

**Dimetrodon** ate small reptiles and amphibians. It had no taste for plants at all. **Varanosaurus**, a lizard-like reptile, was nimble on its feet. But it did not stand a chance against a hungry **Dimetrodon**.

Even smaller than **Varanosaurus** was the amphibian **Seymouria** (SEE-MORE-EE-AH), shown here dashing away from danger.

# carnivore

**Seymouria** was about the length of a small dog, and it had sharp teeth in a wide mouth. Nevertheless, it would find it hard, like **Varanosaurus**, to defend itself against a predatory **Dimetrodon**.

Fortunately for this **Seymouria**, **Dimetrodon** was already feasting. But he would soon have an appetite again and start to hunt another victim.

When scientists first discovered the teeth of **Dimetrodon**, they knew right away that the animal must have been a meat-eater. Teeth always provide a good clue to an animal's feeding habits.

**Dimetrodon**'s jaws were lined with many large, sharp teeth. And, at the very front, it had particularly long ones, like the canine teeth of today's wolves and larger dogs.

# In Permian

**Dimetrodon** lived during what scientists call Early Permian (PER-MEE-YAN) times — that's about 280 million years before humans, and even before the arrival of dinosaurs. It probably spent most of its day in forest clearings or on beaches by inland seas or lakes. It would bask in the sun when temperatures were not too hot. Experts have found many **Dimetrodon** skeletal remains near what appears to be a lake that occasionally dried up.

The climate was gradually becoming warmer in Early Permian times. There was less rainfall than there had previously been, and seasons had started to become more distinct.

Reptiles like **Dimetrodon** were well adapted for these changes. The sail-like structures on their backs helped them cope with the changing temperatures and extreme heat of a Permian afternoon, as you are about to discover.

# Not too hot,

Ever since **Dimetrodon** remains were first dug up about a hundred years ago, scientists have been arguing about the function of the animal's sail-like structure. Now, however, they have come up with the most likely answer.

Like other cold-blooded creatures, reptiles have to rely on sources of heat from outside their bodies.

**Dimetrodon**'s sail probably acted as a temperature-control system. Even though the climate was generally warming up, the air was still very chilly in the Early Permian mornings. If **Dimetrodon** stood with its sail facing the sun, blood vessels in the sail would soon heat up to warm **Dimetrodon**.

# not too cold

No longer chilly, **Dimetrodon** would feel energetic enough to chase after a victim for breakfast.

Later in the day, when the sun was strong and **Dimetrodon** had built up more body heat, it could position itself so that the sail faced a different direction.

Less heat would be taken in this way, cooling **Dimetrodon** down.

The two illustrations show how **Dimetrodon** may have positioned itself at different times during the day to control its body temperature. Which do you think was its early morning position?

# Skeletal

Take a look at this drawing of a **Dimetrodon** skeleton. The head and jaws are striking. The teeth are very long and sharp at the front. Just imagine how powerful these animals must have been! Any victim of this ferocious carnivore barely stood a chance.

But most noticeable of all are the long spines sticking up from the skeleton's back. These were covered with skin. This structure helped control **Dimetrodon**'s body temperature. But it is possible that the sail was also useful in attracting a mate. In addition, the huge size of the sail may have frightened enemies and put fear into prey.

# remains

As you can see, **Dimetrodon**'s legs were somewhat sprawled, ending in clawed toes. It probably waddled along. Its hind legs were a little smaller than its forelimbs.

The bones making up **Dimetrodon**'s tail got smaller and smaller toward the end. Try counting them.

Scientists classify creatures like **Dimetrodon** in a group called pelycosaurs (PELL-ICK-OH-SORZ). Some had sails just like **Dimetrodon**. They were among the most advanced land animals of Early Permian times. Turn the page to meet another pelycosaur. Later, you will meet some dinosaurs that had similar sails.

# Another

Edaphosaurus (EDD-AF-OH-SAW-RUS), like **Dimetrodon**, was not a dinosaur but a reptile. It belonged to a group that scientists call pelycosaurs. It was very much like **Dimetrodon** in appearance, too.

**Edaphosaurus** was about the same size as **Dimetrodon**, or just a little bigger.

In one way, **Edaphosaurus** was quite different from **Dimetrodon**. It was a harmless herbivore, eating only leaves and other vegetation. It did not eat other creatures.

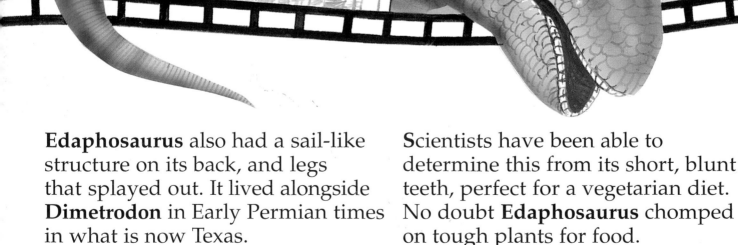

**Edaphosaurus** also had a sail-like structure on its back, and legs that splayed out. It lived alongside **Dimetrodon** in Early Permian times in what is now Texas.

Scientists have been able to determine this from its short, blunt teeth, perfect for a vegetarian diet. No doubt **Edaphosaurus** chomped on tough plants for food.

# pelycosaur

Carnivores like **Dimetrodon** had very different-looking teeth. They ripped chunks of flesh from their prey.

Scientists have also found that the spines making up **Edaphosaurus**'s sail-like structure were rougher than those of **Dimetrodon**'s sail. This may have made **Edaphosaurus**'s temperature control system more efficient.

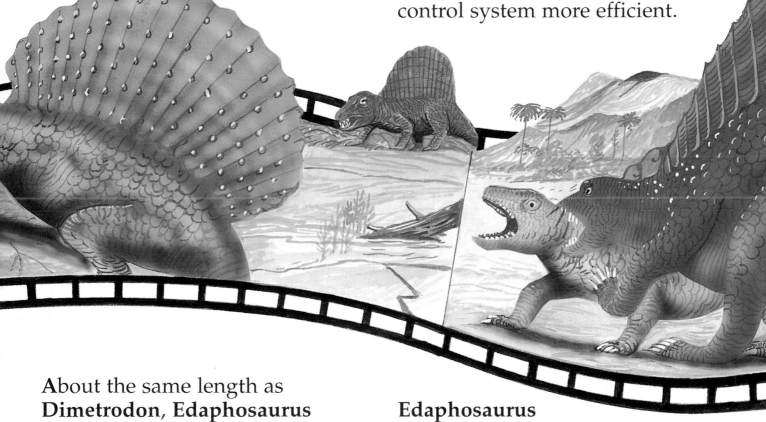

About the same length as **Dimetrodon, Edaphosaurus** probably had to take in large quantities of vegetation in order to keep up its energy. It probably spent most of the Permian day simply eating and resting.

**Edaphosaurus** needed an efficient system to keep it alert in case of attack by carnivorous reptiles, such as **Dimetrodon**!

# Dinosaurs

Although they evolved millions of years after **Dimetrodon** became extinct, a few types of dinosaurs also had sails on their backs. One of these was **Spinosaurus** (SPINE-OH-SAW-RUS), *below*.

**Spinosaurus** was an enormous meat-eating dinosaur that lived in what is now Africa. The longest of the spines that supported its sail were the height of a fully grown human today.

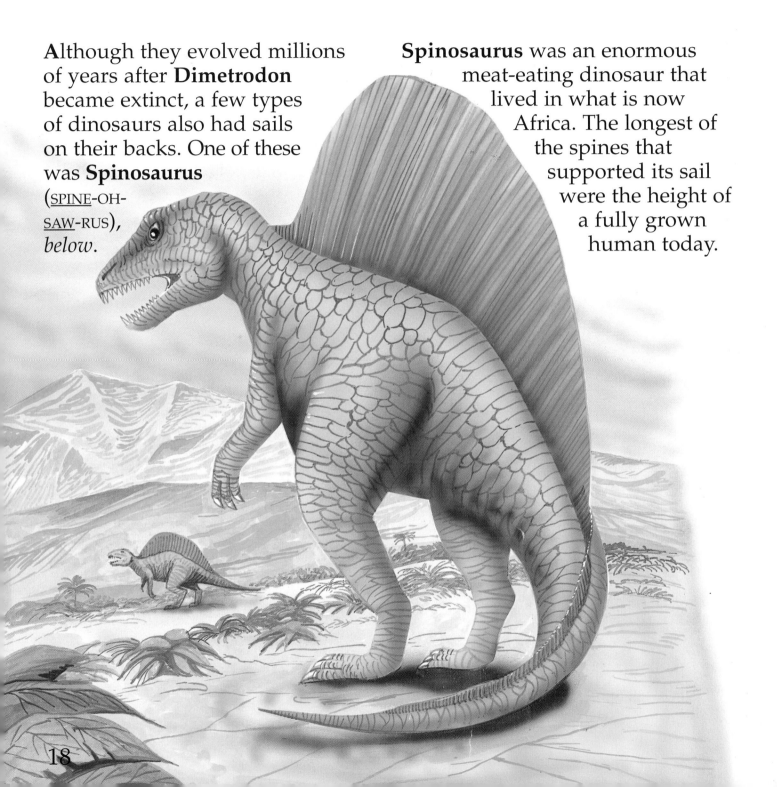

# with "sails"

**Ouranosaurus** (OO-<u>RAN</u>-OH-<u>SAW</u>-RUS), *below*, was another dinosaur with a sail on its back. Its remains have also been dug up in Africa. But, unlike **Spinosaurus**, it was an herbivore.

**Altispinax** (AL-TEE-<u>SPINE</u>-ACKS), *below*, was a carnivore that lived in Europe before **Spinosaurus**'s time. Along **Altispinax**'s back, there was a sail, too, although a small one. Scientists think dinosaur "sails" had much the same purpose as **Dimetrodon**'s sail — the regulation of body temperature.

# Other Permian

Let's get to know a few of the other creatures that shared the Permian world. Smaller than **Dimetrodon**, and living at the same time, was **Diadectes** (DIE-ADD-ECT-EES), *below*. It was quite heavily built and had a rounded snout.

**Diadectes**'s teeth have been described as peglike. They show that the animal was an herbivore. Its legs were very short and thick, as you can see, *below left*. Scientists think that it may have been able to swim.

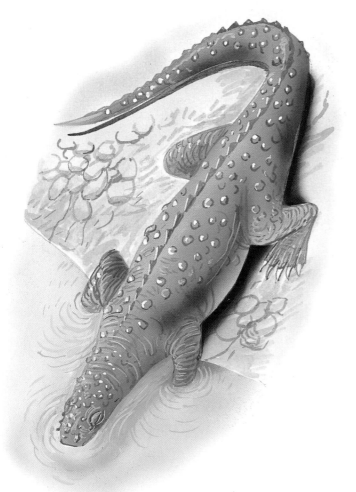

**Varanosaurus**, *above*, had a high, narrow skull, long snout, and teeth that were small and spiky. Experts believe it was a fish-eater. Only about 3 feet (1 m) long, it was smaller and slimmer than most other Early Permian reptiles. It was also more agile.

# creatures

Elginia (<u>ELL</u>-<u>GIN</u>-EE-AH), *below*, another Late Permian reptile, lived, like **Sauroctonus**, in what is now Europe. It had small hornlike growths around its skull and knobby body armor. Its teeth were peglike, which indicates it probably was a plant-eater.

**By** Late Permian times — several million years later but still well before the dinosaurs evolved — even more unusual reptiles roamed parts of the planet. **Sauroctonus** (<u>SORE</u>-OCT-<u>OH</u>-NUS), *above*, had huge canine teeth on both its upper and lower jaws, clearly making it a meat-eater. Its legs were fairly long for a reptile, so it may have been a fast runner.

# Dimetrodon data

Dimetrodon is, of course, best known for its extraordinary sail. Scientists are unsure how heavy this structure was, but it was definitely very useful in keeping **Dimetrodon**'s body temperature at a comfortable level. It was also probably a very attractive body feature to others of its kind, making **Dimetrodon** look powerful and majestic to mates.

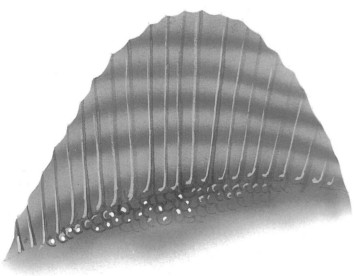

### Strong bite

**Dimetrodon**'s other main feature was its strong bite. The pointed teeth at the front of its mouth were perfect for biting into the flesh of unlucky victims. Its big and strong jaws were excellent for chewing the raw meat. Few small reptiles would have stood a chance against **Dimetrodon** when it was hungry and on the lookout for a tasty meal.

## Slow mover

**Dimetrodon**'s tail was almost the same length as the rest of its body. It was tapered, getting thinner toward the tip. **Dimetrodon**'s tail was possibly quite heavy. This fact, together with the sail, may have slowed **Dimetrodon** down as it moved.

## Leathery skin

No one knows for sure what color **Dimetrodon** was because it is impossible to judge from its

fossilized remains. But scientists think that its skin was fairly tough and leathery, and may have had a scaly appearance.

## Chunky legs

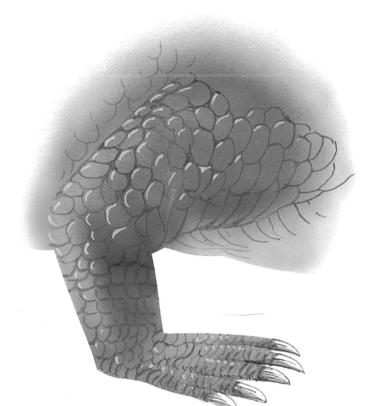

If you flip back through this book, you'll also see how **Dimetrodon**'s chunky legs stuck out from its body at an awkward angle and ended in five-toed feet. The claws at the end of its toes no doubt helped **Dimetrodon** grip the ground as it walked. They may have come in handy, too, for attacking prey. All in all, does **Dimetrodon** remind you of any of today's creatures? If **Dimetrodon** had longer jaws and no sail on its back, wouldn't it be similar to a giant crocodile?

# Glossary

**agile** — able to move easily and quickly.

**amphibians** — creatures that can live on land or in water. Frogs, toads, newts, and salamanders are well-known amphibians.

**carnivores** — living beings that eat meat.

**cold-blooded** — having a body temperature that changes according to the temperature of the surroundings.

**Edaphosaurus** — a large, plant-eating pelycosaur that lived 260 million years ago during Early Permian times, in what is now North America.

**herbivores** — living beings that eat plants.

**pelycosaurs** — prehistoric reptiles that had "sails" on their backs to control body temperature and possibly to attract mates.

**Permian Times** — a time on Earth from 290 – 245 million years ago, before dinosaurs or humans appeared on Earth.

**reptiles** — a group of cold-blooded animals that includes pelycosaurs and dinosaurs from the past; as well as today's lizards, snakes, and crocodiles.

**Seymouria** — an amphibian from Permian times that had sharp teeth and was about the length of a small dog.

# Index